NATIONAL GEOGRAPHIC

D0503671

Spring, Summer, Fall, Winter

David Tunkin

It is spring.

The spring months are March, April, and May.

It is summer.

The summer months are June, July, and August.

It is Fall.

The fall months are September, October, and November.

It is winter.

The winter months are December, January, and February.

Look at the calendar.
It shows the spring, summer, fall, and winter months.

January

February

March

April | May | June

July

August

September

October

November

December

Which picture shows spring? Summer? Fall? Winter?